Neymar

The Complete Story of a Football Superstar

100+ Interesting Trivia Questions, Interactive Activities, and Random, Shocking Fun Facts Every "Ney" Fan Needs to Know

© COPYRIGHT 2023 – HOUSE OF BALLERS – ALL RIGHTS RESERVED.

The content contained within this book may not be reproduced, duplicated, or transmitted without direct written permission from the author or the publisher.

Under no circumstances will any blame or legal responsibility be held against the publisher, or author, for any damages, reparation, or monetary loss due to the information contained within this book. Either directly or indirectly.

Legal Notice:

This book is copyright protected. This book is only for personal use. You cannot amend, distribute, sell, use, quote or paraphrase any part of the content within this book without the consent of the author or publisher.

Disclaimer Notice:

Please note the information contained within this document is for educational and entertainment purposes only. All effort has been executed to present accurate, up-to-date, and reliable, complete information. No warranties of any kind are declared or implied. Readers acknowledge that the author is not engaging in the rendering of legal, financial, medical or professional advice. The content within this book has been derived from various sources.

YOUR FREE BONUS!

The 11 Most Iconic Moments in Football History

In this special edition, you'll discover the secret stories behind them.

Enjoy!

>>SCAN THE QR CODE BELOW TO GAIN EXCLUSIVE ACCESS<<

Contents

Introduction 5

    Chapter 1: Birth & Childhood 7

    Chapter 2: Foray Into Football & Youth Career 14

    Chapter 3: Breakthrough At Santos Fc & Move To Barcelona 21

    Chapter 4: Glory Years At Barcelona 29

    Chapter 5: World Record Transfer To Psg 36

    Chapter 6: International Career 43

    Chapter 7: Profile & Style Of Play 51

    Chapter 8: Career Achievements & Individual Accolades 58

    Chapter 9: Personal Life & Philanthropy 65

    Chapter 10: Notable Off-Field Events 72

Puzzle Solutions 79

Final Whistle 90

INTRODUCTION

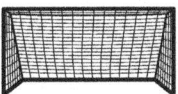

Pelé, Zico, Romario, Roberto Carlos, Rivaldo, Ronaldo Delima…Brazil has always had a conveyor belt of world-class superstars. In fact, no other country in the world has a bigger football heritage and culture than Brazil.

So, making a mark as one of the most talented players to emerge from a football-crazy country like Brazil is no mean feat.

Yet, Neymar da Silva Santos Junior did not just do that; he has also cemented his standing as the undisputed leader of this generation of Brazilian footballers. The fleet-footed, São Paulo-born footballer overcame his impoverished beginnings and a ghastly car crash as an infant to become one of the best players to ever step onto a football pitch.

Renowned for his dribbling skills, vision, touch, creativity, finishing, tricks and feints, Neymar was dubbed as the natural heir to Ronaldinho while he was still at Santos, and the man to inherit the crown Cristiano Ronaldo and Lionel Messi regularly passed among themselves for more than a decade when he joined Barcelona in 2013. And he has gone a long way to satisfy a lot of the hype around him as a lanky teenager.

Many would argue that Neymar has still not reached his full potential due to his incessant fitness and attitude issues, but the Brazilian footballer has still left an indelible mark everywhere he has played, from Santos to Barcelona to PSG and the Brazilian national team where he recently became joint-highest goalscorer alongside football legend and icon, Pelé.

Neymar has faced a lot of criticism during his career and has responded admirably well on plenty of occasions, most notably when he inspired Brazil to succeed at the

Neymar

2013 FIFA Confederations Cup and the 2016 Summer Olympics. He is also credited for playing a starring role in Barcelona's treble success in 2015, its domestic double in 2016, and that historic comeback against PSG in 2017.

Neymar is the eighth player to lift both the Copa Libertadores and the UEFA Champions League and the first to score in final triumphs in both competitions. He was also the first player to score 20 goals for two different sides in European Cup and Champions League history.

Do you want to know more about arguably the most exciting Brazilian player of the past decade? Do you want to know a bit more about the most expensive footballer of all time? If yes, then you have picked up the right book.

If watching Neymar take on his opponents gives you a thrill, then the contents of this book will also leave you on the edge of your seat. The book captures his illustrious career in detail. From his futsal origins, through his audacious skill moves, and down to the controversies he has courted throughout his career, get ready to take a deep dive behind the scenes to know what makes Neymar tick.

So sit back and enjoy some captivating stories, intriguing trivia, and facts about Neymar, the exciting boy-wonder from the land of *o jogo bonito*.

CHAPTER 1
BIRTH & CHILDHOOD

"My father has been by my side since I was little. He takes care of things, my finances, and my family."

- Neymar

Neymar

Neymar da Silva Santos Junior was born on 5 February 1992 in Mogi das Cruzes, on the outskirts of the state of Sao Paulo, Brazil. His mother, Nadine Gonçalves and father, Neymar Santos Sr., lived an impoverished life prior to his birth, as they could not even afford an ultrasound scan to check Neymar's health status during the pregnancy. Neymar was the first of two children his parents had. His only sibling is his younger sister, Rafaella Santos. His father played as an amateur footballer in Brazil's lowest football division.

While he was only four months old, Neymar, in the company of his parents, survived a ghastly car accident on their way to visit some relatives. Neymar escaped any fractures but suffered terrible bruises, while his father dislocated his hip bone. Neymar's mother was not badly hurt and was able to remove herself from the vehicle through the smashed windshield. The family got help from people nearby, and Neymar and his father were removed from the vehicle and taken to a hospital, where they received the required medical attention and eventually recuperated. Neymar Sr. never fully recovered from the hip injury, which led to a premature end to his football career.

Neymar grew up alongside his sister, Rafaella Santos, who was born three years after the accident. Early signs of what Neymar was going to become began to show through the way he kicked things, such as his favourite balloon. He was enrolled on a school that suited his footballing aspirations. He balanced his passion for football with going to school at first before the attainment of professional status prompted him to set aside his studies and focus solely on football.

10 Trivia Questions

1. In which Brazilian state was Neymar born?

    A. Rio de Janeiro

    B. Belo Horizonte

    C. São Paulo

    D. Fortaleza

2. How many siblings does Neymar have?

    A. 1

    B. 2

    C. 3

    D. 4

3. How old was Neymar when he was involved in a car accident?

    A. 14 months

    B. 4 months

    C. 4 years

    D. 24 months

4. What sport was Neymar's father involved in prior to the accident?

    A. Netball

    B. Volleyball

    C. Basketball

    D. Football

5. How many fractures were sustained by Neymar in the accident?

    A. 0

    B. 4

    C. 2

    D. 3

6. In which month was Neymar born?

    A. January

    B. February

    C. December

    D. April

7. What is the first name of Neymar's mother?

    A. Natalie

    B. Madeline

    C. Nadine

    D. Nadiya

8. What was Neymar's favourite childhood hobby?

    A. Playing video games

    B. Watching movies

    C. Traveling

    D. Playing football/kicking things

9. From whom did Neymar inherit his name?

    A. His father

    B. His grandfather

    C. His uncle

    D. His great-grandfather

10. What is the name of Neymar's sister?

    A. Raquel

    B. Rafaella

    C. Roseline

    D. Renata

10 Trivia Answers

1. C – São Paulo
2. A – 1
3. B – 4 months
4. D – Football
5. A – 0
6. B – February
7. C – Nadine
8. D – Playing football
9. A – His father
10. B – Rafaella

NEYMAR JR. MAZE #1

GOAL

CHAPTER 2
FORAY INTO FOOTBALL & YOUTH CAREER

"The 18-year-old (Neymar) is a magnificent prospect. He is sleek and skilful, able to beat the defender on either side, capable of combining well, and full of tricks he can put to productive use in and around the penalty area."

- Tim Vickery

Among his childhood hobbies, Neymar cherished playing football the most. His father recognized his incredible talent at an early age and vowed to help his son fulfil his potential. Neymar began combining futsal with street football at the age of 6. It helped him develop quick thinking, superb technique, and the ability to work with the ball in small spaces.

In order to secure greater opportunities for more competitive futsal engagements for Neymar, his family moved from Mogi das Cruzes to Sao Vicente in 1999. He passed a trial and was inducted into the futsal youth ranks of Portuguesa Santista. After watching him play for the first time, fans were impressed with his array of skills and instantly named him "a child phenomenon" as he used his array of feints and tricks to get past players bigger and older than he was.

Neymar's star shone brightly, earning him a move to Santos F.C in 2003. The lucrative contract he got significantly improved the financial condition of his family, with whom he moved to Santos. The family bought their first house near Vila Belmiro, Santos FC's home ground, and regularly blessed Neymar for helping them escape abject poverty.

While at Santos, Neymar began to attract the attention of scouts from top European clubs, and he was invited for a trial with Real Madrid in 2006. He travelled with his father to Spain, but a deal for his transfer was not agreed upon as his father was not impressed with Real Madrid's offer. His father decided it was best he continued to grow with Santos. The Brazilian club raised Neymar's wage from 10,000 to 125,000 reals per month to ward off interest in the talented teenager. He met Paulo Henrique Ganso while at Santos FC's academy, and the two became good friends.

Neymar's performances for Santos' youth team earned him a call-up to Brazil's under-17 youth side, where he became a close friend of Phillippe Coutinho. When Neymar turned 17, he was promoted to Santos' first team and rewarded with a first professional contract.

10 Trivia Questions

1. At what age did Neymar start playing futsal?

    A. 9

    B. 10

    C. 12

    D. 6

2. On what surface is futsal played?

    A. Grass

    B. Hard court

    C. Sand

    D. Clay

3. When did Neymar and his family leave Mogi das Cruzes?

    A. 1997

    B. 2002

    C. 1999

    D. 2001

4. What was the name of Neymar's futsal club in São Vicente?

    A. Portuguesa Santista

    B. Aquarius Futsal

    C. Campo Mourão Futsal

    D. Carlos Barbosa

5. When did Neymar move to Santos FC?

   A. 2000

   B. 2001

   C. 2005

   D. 2003

6. Which famous Spanish club offered Neymar a trial while he was at Santos?

   A. FC Barcelona

   B. Real Madrid CF

   C. Valencia CF

   D. Atletico Madrid

7. When did Neymar visit Spain for a trial with a Spanish club?

   A. 2003

   B. 2005

   C. 2006

   D. 2007

8. How old was Neymar when he signed his first professional contract with Santos FC?

   A. 17

   B. 20

   C. 19

   D. 16

9. When was Neymar promoted to the first team of Santos FC?

   A. 2006

   B. 2007

   C. 2008

   D. 2009

10. Which former Brazil international footballer did Neymar meet at Santos FC's academy and became good friends with?

    A. Juninho

    B. Ganso

    C. Pato

    D. Kaka

10 Trivia Answers

1. D – 6
2. B – Hard court
3. C – 1999
4. A – Portuguesa Santista
5. D – 2003
6. B – Real Madrid
7. C – 2006
8. A – 17
9. D – 2009
10. B – Ganso

NEYMAR JR. WORD SCRAMBLE #1

1. AZBILR OATNALNI TAEM _____
2. OAJG NIBOOT _____
3. EVFI SATR LILSKS _____
4. PCONAMIHS GLAEUE _____
5. EANYRM AD IAVLS SOSNAT NUIRJO _____
6. SPAINHS AL AGIL _____
7. ILUS EAUSZR _____
8. LODRW UPC IALFN _____
9. SOEALEC BLAIRSIEAR _____
10. LONEIL IESSM _____
11. OMPLSICY _____
12. CF RNALEACOB _____
13. SPAIR ISNTA EGANIRM _____
14. DRNSAE SNIEATI _____
15. IAVX ANEZNHDER _____
16. UEILG NU _____
17. OSASNT CF _____
18. NOIODHLANR _____
19. IIVNUCIS OINURJ _____
20. OCASV AD AAMG _____

CHAPTER 3
BREAKTHROUGH AT SANTOS FC & MOVE TO BARCELONA

"Neymar is growing into a crescendo, and he will soon be considered one of the best in the world. Technically, he has all the skills."

– *Thiago Silva*

Neymar

Neymar made his debut for the first team of Santos FC on 7 March 2009, coming on as a second-half substitute in a 2-1 win over Oeste. He scored his first goal a week later against Mogi Mirim and also scored the winner in a 2-1 win over Palmeiras in the first leg of the Campeonato Paulista semifinal. He ended his debut season in the first team with 14 goals in 48 games.

Neymar's rise continued in the following season, scoring 5 goals in an 8-1 win over Guarani on 15 April 2010. He scored 14 goals in 19 games to help Santos to succeed in the 2010 Campeonato Paulista and was named the competition's best player. Neymar finished his second season with 42 goals in 60 games and soon began to draw comparisons to notable Brazilian footballers like Robinho and Pele.

Santos rejected bids for Neymar from English Premier League clubs West Ham United and Chelsea in 2010, and the player himself reiterated his desire to remain focused on Santos. His agent, Wagner Ribeiro, however, stated that Neymar needed to leave Brazil in order to become the best player in the world. Despite picking up a reputation for diving and an alleged attitude problem, Neymar was voted third best in the 2010 South American Footballer of the Year awards, behind Andres D'Alessandro and Juan Sebastian Veron.

Neymar scored seven goals, including one in the final against Penarol, to help Santos win the 2011 Copa Libertadores, their first since 1963 when Pele was playing for the club. In September of the same year, Santos president Luis Ribeiro threatened to report Real Madrid to FIFA for trying to sign Neymar to a pre-contract behind Santos' back.

Neymar agreed on a contract extension with Santos to remain at the club until 2014, a deal that reportedly increased his wages by 50%. Neymar scored the opening goal of Santos' 3-1 win over Kashima Reysol in the 2011 FIFA World Club Cup semi-final but was largely subdued in the final as Santos lost 4-0 to his future club Barcelona. He was awarded the 2011 South American Footballer of the Year award and the 2011 FIFA Puskas award for a solo effort he scored in a 5-4 loss to Flamengo in the Brazilian Serie A.

On his 20th birthday on 5 February 2012, Neymar scored the 100th goal of his professional career against Palmerias in the Campeonato Paulista. He ended the 2012 Campeonato Paulista with 20 goals and was named Best Forward and Best Player as Santos was crowned the winner. He finished the 2012 Copa Libertadores as the joint top scorer with 8 goals, but Santos crashed out in the semifinal to eventual winners Corinthians.

Neymar also ended the 2012 Campeonato Brasileiro Serie A with 14 goals and was voted Best Forward. He was also named Best Player of the 2012 Recopa Sudamericana after scoring a goal in a 2-0 aggregate win over Universidad de Chile.

In March 2013, Neymar publicly disclosed his desire to play in Europe for a big club like Barcelona, Real Madrid, or Chelsea. A month later, his representatives revealed that he intended to leave Santos before the 2014 World Cup. Neymar played his final game for Santos on 26 May 2013 and announced his decision to join Barcelona the following day. He signed a 5-year contract with the Spanish club and was unveiled to media and fans on 3 June 2013.

10 Trivia Questions

1. When did Neymar make his Santos first-team debut?

    A. January 2010

    B. January 2009

    C. March 2009

    D. April 2011

2. Against which team did Neymar make his first team debut at Santos?

    A. Palmeiras

    B. Oeste

    C. Mogi Mirim

    D. Botafogo

3. Against which team did Neymar score his first senior goal for Santos?

    A. Mogi Mirim

    B. Oeste

    C. Palmeiras

    D. Flamengo

4. How many goals did Neymar score in his first season with Santos' senior team?

    A. 11

    B. 9

    C. 23

    D. 14

5. Against which team did Neymar score 5 goals in April 2010?

   A. Atletico Mineiro

   B. Botafogo

   C. Guarani

   D. Palmeiras

6. How many appearances did Neymar make in his second senior season at Santos?

   A. 35

   B. 60

   C. 25

   D. 50

7. How many goals did Neymar score in the 2011 Copa Libertadores?

   A. 7

   B. 8

   C. 9

   D. 10

8. Against which team did Neymar score the 100th goal of his senior career?

   A. Penarol

   B. Kashiwa Reysol

   C. Palmeiras

   D. Flamengo

9. Which team tried signing Neymar to a pre-contract in 2011?

   A. Barcelona

   B. Real Madrid

   C. Chelsea

   D. West Ham United

10. Against which team did Neymar play his final game for Santos?

    A. Flamengo

    B. Sao Bernardo

    C. Botafogo

    D. Union Barbarense

10 Trivia Answers

1. C – March 2009
2. B – Oeste
3. A – Mogi Mirim
4. D – 14
5. C – Guarani
6. B – 60
7. A – 7
8. C – Palmeiras
9. B – Real Madrid
10. A – Flamengo

Neymar

NEYMAR JR. WORD SEARCH #1

```
N A J O G A B O N I T O M A Z
E P Q L P C E C F T S D S G I
Y B R A Z B R A Z I L R R I R
M W P L T R I Q W U O I Y T R
A T X I K R W Q O P T B C M R
R M Y G G P N P R M M B E O R
J F F A V G S K L O K L X Q U
R U Y N X J A C D H E E L C A
O L Y M P I C S C A N R G G W
K S K I L L S Z U W F A K A C
S E L E C A O U P K A W R T R
G B B A R C E L O N A I F V F
K J Q K T C W X Z S U M U W N
C H A M P I O N S J X X L Q Y
V A T O O G N Q U P V Y K O T
```

BRAZIL	CHAMPIONS	WORLDCUP	OLYMPICS
JOGABONITO	NEYMARJR	SELECAO	BARCELONA
SKILLS	LALIGA	MOHAWK	DRIBBLER

CHAPTER 4
GLORY YEARS AT BARCELONA

"He (Neymar) has numbers [which show he is] a beast of a footballer, he's one of the most unbalancing players in the world [for opposition defences], and his signing by this club was a great decision."

- Luis Enrique

Neymar

Neymar made his debut for Barcelona on 30 July 2013 in a 2-2 pre-season friendly draw against Lechia Gdansk and scored his first goal for the club in another friendly against Thailand XI on 7 August. He made his official debut in a 7-0 La Liga win over Levante, coming on as a substitute for Alexis Sanchez, and scored his first competitive goal in a 1-1 draw at Atletico in the Supercopa de Espana first leg. He won his first trophy with Barca following a goalless draw in the second leg of the tie, as Barcelona triumphed on away goals. He played in the UEFA Champions League for the first time on 18 September, setting up one of the goals as Barcelona beat Ajax 4-0. His first goals in the competition were scored on December 11, as he hit a hattrick in a 6-1 victory over Celtic. He finished his first season at the club with 15 goals in 41 appearances across all competitions.

In his second season at Barcelona, Neymar scored 39 goals in 51 appearances across all competitions to help Barcelona to a treble of La Liga, Copa del Rey, and UEFA Champions League. He also finished as the joint-top goalscorer in the Champions League with 10 goals. He helped the club retain both La Liga and Copa del Rey in 2015/16, chipping in with 31 goals in 49 appearances across all competitions.

In the 2016/17 season, Neymar scored two and set up Sergi Roberto's goal in injury time to help Barcelona beat PSG 6-1 to overturn a huge 4-0 first-leg deficit in the UEFA Champions League Round of 16. He scored his 100th goal for Barcelona in a 4-1 victory over Granada. In what eventually became his final appearance for the club, Neymar scored his 105th goal in his 186th appearance for Barcelona to help beat Alaves 3-1 and clinch a third consecutive Copa del Rey title. He left Barcelona in August 2017 for a world record fee, having won eight trophies in his 4-year stay at the club.

10 Trivia Questions

1. Against which team did Neymar make his official Barcelona debut?

    A. Levante

    B. Atletico Madrid

    C. Sevilla

    D. Athletic Bilbao

2. When did Neymar make his first-ever Barcelona appearance?

    A. 20 July 2012

    B. 18 August 2013

    C. 1 August 2011

    D. 10 August 2013

3. Against which team did Neymar score his first competitive Barcelona goal?

    A. Levante

    B. Alaves

    C. Atletico Madrid

    D. Real Valladolid

4. What was Neymar's first trophy with Barcelona?

    A. FIFA Club World Cup

    B. UEFA Super Cup

    C. Copa del Rey

    D. Supercopa de Espana

5. Against which team did Neymar score his first UEFA Champions League goal?

   A. Ajax

   B. Celtic

   C. Manchester City

   D. AC Milan

6. How many appearances did Neymar make in his first season at Barcelona?

   A. 41

   B. 40

   C. 29

   D. 38

7. How many goals did Neymar score in the 2014/15 season?

   A. 37

   B. 38

   C. 39

   D. 40

8. Against which team did Neymar score his 100th Barcelona goal?

   A. Levante

   B. Elche

   C. Eibar

   D. Granada

9. How many trophies did Neymar win at Barcelona?

   A. 9

   B. 8

   C. 10

   D. 11

10. When did Neymar leave Barcelona?

   A. August 2017

   B. July 2017

   C. June 2017

   D. May 2017

10 Trivia Answers

1. A – Levante
2. B – 18 August 2013
3. C – Atletico Madrid
4. D – Supercopa de España
5. B – Celtic
6. A – 41
7. C – 39
8. D – Granada
9. B – 8
10. A – January 2017

NEYMAR JR. WORD SCRAMBLE #2

1. ANRYEM RJ _____
2. LAEABCNOR _____
3. SPIRA N-GAASETMINR _____
4. STNASO _____
5. EHRTIG-FOTDO _____
6. RDEEMIIFLD _____
7. IRNEWG _____
8. WDAFRRO _____
9. AZLIBR _____
10. NRMLAIOILEI _____

CHAPTER 5
WORLD RECORD TRANSFER TO PSG

"Neymar has reached a point of maturity. What he's doing now puts him on a level with the two other footballers we consider above the rest."

- *Tata Martino*

On 3 August 2017, French Ligue 1 club PSG paid 222 million euros to Barcelona through Neymar's legal representatives, an amount equal to the release clause in his contract for his transfer to the Paris-based club. He penned a 5-year contract that would last until 2022 and was offered the number 10 shirt by Javier Pastore as a welcome gesture.

Neymar made his debut for PSG in a 3-0 Ligue 1 win over Guingamp, in which he scored a goal and provided an assist. He also scored in each of his two UEFA Champions League games for PSG against Celtic and Bayern Munich, respectively. His first season at the club ended prematurely on 26 February 2018 when he fractured his fifth metatarsal bone. He had scored 28 goals in 30 appearances in all competitions before the injury and won the Ligue 1, Coupe de France, and Coupe de la Ligue in his first season at PSG.

In the 2018/19 season, Neymar scored a hattrick against Red Star Belgrade in a Champions League group stage game but missed the Round of 16 tie against Manchester United due to a foot injury and incurred a 3-match ban from UEFA for insulting officials as a penalty was awarded against his side in injury time. Neymar scored in the 2019 Coupe de France final against Rennes, but the game ended in defeat for PSG as Rennes equalized and won on penalties. Neymar finished the season with 23 goals in 28 appearances and won a second successive league title.

In a shortened 2019/20 league season as a result of the COVID-19 pandemic, Neymar won his third straight Ligue1 title and scored the winning goal in a 1-0 win over Saint-Etienne in the Coupe de France final. He also converted his spot kick in the 6-5 penalty shootout win over Lyon in the Coupe de la Ligue final to complete a second domestic treble in three seasons and helped PSG to a first-ever Champions League final, which ended in a 1-0 loss to Bayern Munich.

Neymar scored 17 goals in 31 games in the 2020/21 season to help PSG retain the Coupe de France they won the previous season, as they missed out on the Ligue 1 title to Lille. Neymar's former Barcelona teammate Lionel Messi joined PSG ahead of the start of the 2021/22 season, and the pair helped PSG win Ligue 1, with Neymar scoring 13 goals in 28 appearances in all competitions.

10 Trivia Questions

1. Which player offered his jersey number to Neymar?

    A. Julian Draxler

    B. Javier Pastore

    C. Edinson Cavani

    D. Kylian Mbappe

2. Against which team did Neymar make his PSG debut?

    A. Guingamp

    B. Rennes

    C. Lille

    D. Saint-Etienne

3. Against which team did Neymar make his Champions League debut for PSG?

    A. Bayern Munich

    B. Benfica

    C. Celtic

    D. Juventus

4. How many goals did Neymar score in his first season at PSG?

    A. 15

    B. 46

    C. 25

    D. 28

5. How many games did Neymar play in his second season at PSG?

    A. 47

    B. 28

    C. 39

    D. 30

6. How many goals did Neymar score in the 2019/20 Champions League?

    A. 3

    B. 4

    C. 5

    D. 6

7. For which offence was Neymar banned for 3 games in the Champions League?

    A. Violent conduct

    B. Spitting at an opponent

    C. Insulting officials

    D. Getting involved in a brawl

8. Against which team did Neymar score his first hattrick for PSG in the Champions League?

    A. Celtic

    B. Red Star Belgrade

    C. Istanbul Basaksehir

    D. Young Boys

9. How many trophyless seasons has Neymar had at PSG?

    A. 3

    B. 2

    C. 1

    D. 0

10. On how many occasions has Neymar finished a season as Ligue 1 top goalscorer?

    A. 0

    B. 1

    C. 2

    D. 3

10 Trivia Answers

1. B – Javier Pastore
2. A – Guingamp
3. C – Celtic
4. D – 28
5. B – 28
6. A – 3
7. C – Insulting officials
8. B – Red Star Belgrade
9. D – 0
10. A – 0

NEYMAR JR. MAZE #2

GOAL

CHAPTER 6
INTERNATIONAL CAREER

Neymar is a great player, as we can all see. He is the guy that decides a lot of games, a guy that is fundamental on our national team. We give the ball to him, and he sorts it out."

- ***Coutinho***

Neymar

On the back of Neymar's impressive performances for Santos in 2010, Brazil national team greats such as Pele and Romario urged then-national team coach Dunga to include Neymar as part of his 2010 World Cup squad. Dunga stated that Neymar was superbly talented but not experienced enough to warrant inclusion in either the 23-man squad or even the standby list.

Neymar was called up to Brazil's senior national team for the first time on 26 July 2010 by Dunga's successor, Mario Menezes. Neymar was handed his senior Brazil debut on 10 August 2010 in a friendly against the United States. He wore the number 11 jersey and scored a goal in a 2-0 victory for his side. Neymar scored twice in a 2-0 win over Scotland on 27 March 2011, and a banana was thrown onto the pitch after he scored a penalty kick, leading to his post-match complaint about a hostile atmosphere of racism.

Neymar scored 9 goals, including 2 in the final against Uruguay, to help Brazil win the 20011 South American Youth Championship. He also participated in the 2011 Copa America and scored two goals in the group game against Ecuador before Brazil's elimination in the quarterfinal. Neymar was included in Brazil's squad for the London 2012 Olympics, where he scored three goals to help Brazil to a silver medal finish.

Neymar scored his first senior international hat-trick in an 8-0 win over China in September 2012. Nine days later, he scored the winning goal of Brazil's 2-1 win over Argentina in the 2012 Superclasico de las Americas. Neymar was included in Brazil's squad for the 2013 FIFA Confederations Cup held in Brazil and handed the number 10 jersey. He scored the tournament's first goal in a 3-0 win over Japan and scored in the other two group games against Mexico and Italy, respectively. He also scored in the 3-0 final win over Spain and was recognized as the tournament's best player with the Golden Ball award.

Neymar earned his 50th Brazil senior cap in his team's first game of the 2014 World Cup against Croatia, in which he scored twice to give Brazil a 3-1 comeback win. He scored another brace in the final group game against Cameroon and converted his spot kick during the penalty shootout win over Chile in the Round of 16. His tournament ended prematurely as he sustained an injury in the quarterfinal win over Colombia and missed the heavy semifinal loss to Germany and the third-place playoff loss to the Netherlands.

Neymar was made Brazil captain in late 2014 following the return of Dunga as Brazil's head coach, and in October 2014, he scored 4 goals for the first time in his international career as Brazil beat Japan 4-0 in Singapore. Neymar had a goal and assist in Brazil's 2-1 comeback win over Peru in their first game of the 2015 Copa America. He picked up a booking in the second game against Colombia and kicked a ball at Colombia's Pablo Aimero after the game had ended, resulting in a 4-game ban that ruled him out for the remainder of the competition.

Neymar was selected to play for Brazil at the Rio 2016 Olympics and was named the team's captain. He scored four goals in the knockout stages to help Brazil win its first Olympic gold in men's football. Having received intense criticism before and during the tournament for his conduct on and off the pitch, Neymar relinquished the captaincy of the national team.

Neymar was included in Brazil's final squad for the 2018 World Cup and scored his first goal at the tournament in Brazil's second group game against Costa Rica. He scored his second goal of the tournament against Mexico in the Round of 16 but endured yet more World Cup disappointment as Belgium knocked out Brazil in the quarterfinal. Neymar was meant to be part of Brazil's squad for the 2019 Copa America but suffered an ankle injury that ruled him out of the tournament, which Brazil eventually won.

Neymar made his 100th senior international appearance in a friendly against Senegal played in October 2019. A year later, he scored a hattrick against Peru in a 2022 World Cup qualifier to become his country's second all-time highest goalscorer behind Pele. He also scored 2 goals and provided 4 assists to help Brazil reach the final of the 2021 Copa America. He was named joint-best player of the tournament alongside Lionel Messi despite Brazil's 1-0 loss to Argentina in the final.

Neymar became Brazil's all-time highest goalscorer in World Cup qualification matches with his 12th strike in a 2-0 win over Peru in September 2021. He was named in Brazil's final squad for the 2022 World Cup, and his first goal of the tournament against South Korea in the Round of 16 made him the third Brazilian to score in 3 World Cup tournaments, after Pele and Ronaldo. His goal against Croatia in the quarterfinal drew him level with Pele as Brazil's joint-highest all-time goalscorer.

10 Trivia Questions

1. When did Neymar make his senior international debut?

    A. August 2010

    B. July 2011

    C. June 2009

    D. May 2010

2. Against which team did Neymar make his senior international debut?

    A. Mexico

    B. Scotland

    C. USA

    D. China

3. How many goals did Neymar score at the 2011 South American Youth Championship?

    A. 8

    B. 9

    C. 10

    D. 11

4. Against which team did Neymar score his first senior hat-trick for Brazil?

    A. Uruguay

    B. Paraguay

    C. Scotland

    D. China

5. Against which team did Neymar score his first FIFA World Cup goal?

    A. Croatia

    B. Cameron

    C. Costa Rica

    D. South Korea

6. How many Olympic games has Neymar been to?

    A. 4

    B. 0

    C. 2

    D. 1

7. Which of these editions of the Copa America did Neymar miss?

    A. 2021 Copa America

    B. 2019 Copa America

    C. 2015 Copa America

    D. 2011 Copa America

8. Against which team did Neymar play his 100th senior game for Brazil?

    A. South Africa

    B. Japan

    C. Portugal

    D. Senegal

9. How many senior Brazil caps has Neymar earned so far?

    A. 124

    B. 123

    C. 122

    D. 121

10. Which trophy has Neymar won with Brazil's senior national team?

    A. Copa America

    B. FIFA World Cup

    C. FIFA Confederations Cup

    D. Finallisma

10 Trivia Answers

1. A – August 2010
2. C – USA
3. B – 9
4. D – China
5. A – Croatia
6. C – 2
7. B – 2019 Copa America
8. D – Senegal
9. A – 124
10. C – FIFA Confederations Cup

NEYMAR JR. WORD SEARCH #2

```
W Y F G A B R H K T E Y F P U
B B A U T Z H I H U I M V E X
E L H B R T B P H M W Y A B G
E N R R A I N I E S T A S W G
G D Q A N E G T M P L V C U H
R C V S S U Z H E Y B K O W A
A H E I F L T R S W J N D Z V
V Y R L E Y G Z S E I G A W T
S N R E R K P Z I F P W G U K
U G A I F R S A N T O S A W E
A F T R E L A S P K U F M P N
R T T A E L I G U E U N A E D
E K I O B R R P E N A L T Y W
Z D J J R O N A L D I N H O F
Q L X A V I L Q J I Q R A K F
```

MESSI RONALDINHO BRASILEIRAO VASCODAGAMA
VERRATTI XAVI SANTOS LIGUEUN
SUAREZ PENALTY INIESTA TRANSFERFEE

CHAPTER 7
PROFILE & STYLE OF PLAY

"Neymar is young, though, and I can't explain how special he will become. In the next two or three seasons, he will become the best player."

- Ronaldinho

Neymar

Neymar had incredible promise as a youth player and was tipped to become the best player in the world by former Brazil national team stars like Ronaldo and Ronaldinho. Neymar usually plays as either a winger, supporting striker, lone striker, or sometimes as an attacking midfielder and has been dubbed "a true phenomenon." His status as PSG's sixth-highest goalscorer and seventh-highest assister of all-time shows his remarkable scoring and playmaking abilities. He mostly plays as a left-sided forward for both club and country in a 4-3-3 setup, darting infield on his stronger right foot towards the opposition goal due to his creativity and blistering pace. This enables him to shoot or create an opportunity for a teammate.

Neymar's dribbling skills, flair, playmaking ability, tricks, and feints have led to comparisons between him and Ronaldinho. His core attributes are dribbling, passing, finishing, creativity, feints and tricks, vision, touch, and technique that has been described as "explosive" and "electric.". Neymar is known for performing the rainbow flick on occasion, and he is a prolific goalscorer, capable of finishing with both feet or head despite him being predominantly right-footed. He is also a good freekick and penalty kick taker and has been inspired by accomplished footballers such as Lionel Messi, Cristiano Ronaldo, Wayne Rooney, and Andres Iniesta. Neymar has scored 436 senior career goals, 359 in spells with Santos, Barcelona, and PSG, and 77 for the Brazilian senior national team.

10 Trivia Questions

1. In which role is Neymar usually deployed?

    A. Center-forward

    B. Attacking midfielder

    C. Right-sided forward

    D. Left-sided forward

2. Which player has inspired Neymar?

    A. Julio Baptista

    B. Lionel Messi

    C. Carlos Bacca

    D. Nuno Gomes

3. Which trick is associated with Neymar?

    A. Rainbow flick

    B. Cruyff turn

    C. Maradona turn

    D. Knuckle-ball freekick

4. How many players have scored more goals for PSG than Neymar?

    A. 7

    B. 6

    C. 5

    D. 4

5. For which trait has Neymar received intense criticism?

    A. Dribbling

    B. Shooting

    C. Passing

    D. Diving

6. Which of Neymar's traits has been described as "explosive" and "electric?"

    A. Technique

    B. Tackling

    C. Vision

    D. Heading

7. Which former Brazil international tipped Neymar to become the world's best player?

    A. Juninho

    B. Ronaldinho

    C. Robinho

    D. Kaka

8. How many goals has Neymar scored in his senior career (As of February, 2023)?

    A. 438

    B. 437

    C. 436

    D. 435

9. How many club goals has Neymar scored?

    A. 356

    B. 357

    C. 358

    D. 359

10. How many goals has Neymar scored for Brazil's senior national team?

    A. 77

    B. 76

    C. 75

    D. 74

10 Trivia Answers

1. D – Left-sided forward
2. B – Lionel Messi
3. A – Rainbow flick
4. C – 5
5. D – Diving
6. A – Technique
7. B – Ronaldinho
8. C – 436
9. D – 359
10. A - 77

NEYMAR JR. WORD SCRAMBLE #3

1. AAAFELLR OTNASS _____
2. NLOAARIC ASANDT _____
3. EDANNI OSCGEAVNL _____
4. REAMNY RS _____
5. CJIESAS RNIUIT _____
6. GMOI ASD CEUZRS _____
7. IVAD CCAUL _____
8. OLAFBTLO _____
9. WDROL PUC _____
10. OAPC MCAIEAR _____

CHAPTER 8
CAREER ACHIEVEMENTS & INDIVIDUAL ACCOLADES

"I like Neymar a lot. He is a bit like me. He had some difficulties in getting used to his new environment at first, but I knew that he was going to succeed."

– Cristiano Ronaldo

Neymar has amassed an enviable haul of honours in his accomplished career, especially at the club level. During his time at Santos, he won the Copa Libertadores (2011), Copa do Brasil (2010), Recopa Sudamericana (2012), and Campeonato Paulista (2010, 2011, & 2012). At Barcelona, Neymar won two La Liga titles (2014/15 & 2015/16), three Copa del Rey titles (2014/15, 2015/16, & 2016/17), UEFA Champions League (2014/15), Supercopa de Espana (2013), and FIFA Club World Cup (2015).

Since joining PSG in 2017, Neymar has won four French Ligue 1 titles, three Coupe de France titles, two Coupe de la Ligue titles, and Trophee des Champions on three occasions. He helped Brazil win the 2011 South American U-20 Championship and played a pivotal role in the success of Brazil's under-23 side at the London 2012 and Rio 2016 Olympic games. Neymar was also instrumental in Brazil's success at the 2013 FIFA Confederations Cup and the country's run to the final of the 2021 Copa America.

Neymar has been named to the Campeonato Brasileiro Série A Team of the Year on three occasions and was named the league's best player in 2011. *World Soccer* recognized him as their Young Player of the Year in 2011, the same year he claimed the FIFA Puskas Award. He has also won the Copa Libertadores Most Valuable Player award and FIFA Club World Cup Bronze Ball. Neymar finished third in the 2015 Ballon d'Or, has won Samba Gold 5 times, and was named La Liga Best World Player (2014/15) and UNFP Ligue 1 Player of the Year (2017/18)

Neymar has been named South American Footballer of the Year twice (2011 & 2012), and he picked up the Golden Ball and Bronze Shoe at the 2013 Confederations Cup. He was also named in the FIFA Confederations Cup Dream Team (2013), FIFA World Cup Dream Team (2014), FIF- FIFPro World11 (2015 & 2017), UEFA Team of the Year (2015 & 2020), UEFA Champions League Squad of the Season (2014/15, 2019/20, & 2020/21), UNFP Ligue 1 Team of the Year (2017/18, 2018/19, & 2020/21), and Copa America Team of the Tournament (2021).

10 Trivia Questions

1. When did Neymar win the FIFA Puskas award?

    A. 2009

    B. 2010

    C. 2011

    D. 2007

2. How many times has Neymar won Samba Gold?

    A. 6

    B. 1

    C. 3

    D. 2

3. How many times has Neymar been selected in the FIFA-FIFPro World11?

    A. 1

    B. 2

    C. 3

    D. 4

4. When was Neymar selected in the FIFA World Cup Dream Team?

    A. 2022

    B. 2018

    C. 2010

    D. 2014

5. When did Neymar finish third in the Ballon d'Or?

    A. 2013

    B. 2014

    C. 2015

    D. 2016

6. How many trophies did Neymar win at Barcelona?

    A. 8

    B. 9

    C. 10

    D. 11

7. In which season did Neymar finish as UEFA Champions League joint-top goalscorer?

    A. 2013/14

    B. 2014/15

    C. 2015/16

    D. 2016/17

8. How many times has Neymar been selected in the UEFA Team of the Year?

    A. 5

    B. 4

    C. 3

    D. 2

9. How many times has Neymar been voted South American Footballer of the Year?

    A. 2

    B. 3

    C. 0

    D. 5

10. When was Neymar selected for the Copa America Team of the Tournament?

    A. 2011

    B. 2015

    C. 2021

    D. 2019

10 Trivia Answers

1. C – 2011
2. A – 6
3. B – 2
4. D – 2014
5. C – 2015
6. A – 8
7. B – 2014/15
8. D – 2
9. A – 2
10. C – 2021

NEYMAR JR. CROSSWORD PUZZLE #1

ACROSS

[3] PSG's rival city

[4] His birth country

[7] His dominant foot

[8] First european team

DOWN

[1] His club in Brazil

[2] The highest level of football

[5] The league PSG competes in

[6] His position

CHAPTER 9
PERSONAL LIFE & PHILANTHROPY

"Everyone knows how extraordinarily talented you are, but if they could only see how real and beautiful you are inside your heart. You have all my respect and honour, bebe."

– Natalia Barulich

Neymar

Neymar has an 11-year-old son named Davi Lucca da Silva Santos, whom he had with former girlfriend Carolina Dantas in August 2011. The relationship began in 2010 and ended in 2011, before the birth of their son. Neymar has been involved in the life of his son and provides sufficient resources for the upkeep of the child and his mother. Neymar has also had numerous other relationships and affairs with other women and is currently in a relationship with Natalia Barulich. Neymar also maintains close ties with his sister Rafaella Beckran, whose face he has tattooed on his arm.

Neymar follows the Pentecostal branch of the Christian faith and has occasionally donned a headband with the inscription "100% Jesus." He reportedly tithes his income to the church and has cited Brazilian World Cup winner Kaka as his religious role model.

Neymar lives a lavish lifestyle and possesses two expensive mansions in Rio de Janeiro and Paris, as well as an exquisite collection of cars and wristwatches. He also owns a yacht, a private jet, and a helicopter. He speaks Portuguese and Spanish and is a friendly person who lives a happy life without bothering about the opinions other people have of him.

Neymar was accused of abuse by Brazilian model Najila Trindade, who alleged that the footballer had attacked her in a Paris hotel in May 2019. The case, brought to the São Paulo attorney general's office, was suspended in July 2019 due to lack of evidence. Neymar denied the accusations, alleging that he was being extorted.

Alongside fellow Brazilian footballer Nene, Neymar organizes a charity match annually in Nene's hometown of Jundial. The aim of the charity exhibition is to raise food for families in need.

10 Trivia Questions

1. How old is Neymar's first son?

    A. 14

    B. 11

    C. 10

    D. 6

2. With which woman did Neymar have Davi Lucca?

    A. Natalia Barulich

    B. Najila Trindade

    C. Barbara Evans

    D. Carolina Dantas

3. What is the name of Neymar's current girlfriend?

    A. Najila Trindade

    B. Bruna Marquezine

    C. Natalia Barulich

    D. Elisabeth Martinez

4. What religion does Neymar follow?

    A. Christianity

    B. Islam

    C. Hinduism

    D. Buddhism

5. Which other language does Neymar speak apart from Portuguese?

   A. French

   B. Spanish

   C. Arabic

   D. Malay

6. Which of these women accused Neymar of abuse in 2019?

   A. Janin Ullmann

   B. Thaila Ayala

   C. Laryssa Olivera

   D. Najila Trindade

7. Which Brazilian footballer organizes a charity match alongside Neymar?

   A. Marcelo

   B. Willian

   C. Nene

   D. Oscar

8. Which former Brazil player is Neymar's religious role model?

   A. Kaka

   B. Ronaldo

   C. Adriano

   D. Rivaldo

9. Whose face is tattooed on Neymar's arm?

   A. Davi Lucca dos Santos

   B. Rafaella Beckran

   C. Neymar Sr.

   D. Carolina Dantas

10. Which of these is not among Neymar's possessions?

    A. Mansions

    B. Yacht

    C. Private jet

    D. Submarine

10 Trivia Answers

1. B – 11
2. D – Carolina Dantas
3. C – Natalia Barulich
4. A – Christianity
5. B – Spanish
6. D – Najila Trindade
7. C – Nene
8. A – Kaka
9. B – Rafaella Beckran
10. D – Submarine

NEYMAR JR. WORD SEARCH #3

```
Z Y N I C F G U G J V I R F G
M P E L E R M B X N N Z A M A
E M S N B E X A Y U W T I Z R
J T Z P T E Y L G T F R N N J
G O S A X K R A Z M R J B J I
Y P T C H I J N K E A E O E Q
L S E E U C H C P G I F W N L
T C P S T K S E U G M I F M S
P O O O L E G E N D N V L E Q
S R V K T V Q Z G K L E I B G
P E E Z X H R Y L N O S C L V
E R R R M G Y S A G Z T K S M
E K S U I K V L F C C A I U O
D V B G O E H A L N R R W Q P
W L Y X G A V K U U D S N H B
```

RAINBOWFLICK	PELE	SPEED	STEPOVERS
LEGEND	FREEKICK	FIVESTARS	NUTMEG
BALANCE	MSN	PACE	TOPSCORER

CHAPTER

10

NOTABLE OFF-FIELD EVENTS

"I didn't participate in the negotiations. My father always took care of it and always will. I sign everything he tells me to sign."

- *Neymar*

Neymar has entered into several sponsorship agreements since his stock began to rise from the age of 17. He agreed on an 11-year deal with American sportswear giant Nike in March 2011. The contract was terminated in 2020 after a Nike employee made a sexual assault complaint against Neymar. He is now with German sportswear firm Puma, with whom he agreed to a long-term deal towards the end of 2020. He has also agreed to sponsorship deals with Volkswagen, Lupo, Tenys Pe Baruel, Unilever, Ambev, Claro, and Santander. He was ranked as the world's third-highest paid athlete by Forbes in 2019, with earnings of 105 million dollars.

Neymar was featured on the front covers of North American versions of Pro Evolution Soccer 2012 and Pro Evolution Soccer 2013 after Konami Digital Entertainment disclosed that he had joined the game. He has featured in the EA Sports FIFA video game series, with the trailer of FIFA 18 displaying him in his PSG home kit. He featured alongside Cristiano Ronaldo in the Champions and Ultimate Edition packs for FIFA 19. Neymar's "hang loose" celebration also featured in the game. Neymar became the first Brazilian athlete to feature on the front cover of TIME magazine, appearing in the magazine's February 2013 issue, which included an article by Bobby Ghosh titled "The Next Pele: How the Career of Brazilian football star Neymar Explains his Country's economy."

Neymar has been known to be a promoter of modern Brazilian pop music, especially *Música Sertaneja*. A video in which Neymar is seen dancing in the Santos changing room to the tune of Michel Telo's song *"Ai se eu te pego!"* went viral. He performed dance moves in the song when he scored goals and made an appearance in one of Telo's concerts. He also promoted sertanejo singer Gusttavo Lima, with whom he performed live on the singer's hits *"Balada"* and *"Fazer Beber."* In 2012, Neymar appeared in a music video for another sertanejo hit, *"Eu Quero Tchu, Eu Quero Tcha"* by João Lucas & Marcelo, and in 2013 Neymar featured in a rap music video, *"País do Futebol"* by MC Guimê.

Neymar has also made cameo appearances in a few TV shows and films. He played the role of Monje Joao in *Money Heist* (2019), represented himself in *Os Parcas* (2017), *XXX: Return of Xander Cage* (2017), *The Making of* (2019), *Neymar Jr and the Line of Kings* (2021), and *Neymar: The Perfect Chaos* (2022).

In the 2022 Brazilian general elections, Neymar publicly supported incumbent president Jair Bolsonaro for re-election to a second term in office.

10 Trivia Questions

1. Which sportswear company gave Neymar his first sponsorship deal?

    A. Adidas

    B. New Balance

    C. Nike

    D. Puma

2. When did Neymar agree to a sponsorship deal with Puma?

    A. 2017

    B. 2018

    C. 2015

    D. 2020

3. When was Neymar featured on the cover of TIME magazine?

    A. January 2013

    B. February 2013

    C. March 2013

    D. April 2013

4. How many Brazilian athletes made the cover of TIME magazine before Neymar?

    A. 0

    B. 4

    C. 2

    D. 3

5. When did Neymar first feature on the cover of Pro Evolution Soccer?

    A. 2010

    B. 2011

    C. 2012

    D. 2013

6. In which edition of EA Sports FIFA game was Neymar's "hang loose" celebration featured?

    A. 2016

    B. 2017

    C. 2018

    D. 2019

7. When did Neymar's Nike sponsorship end?

    A. 2019

    B. 2020

    C. 2021

    D. 2022

8. What was Neymar's rank in the 2019 Forbes list of highest paid athletes?

    A. First

    B. Second

    C. Third

    D. Fourth

9. In which year did Neymar support Jair Bolsonaro in Brazil's general elections?

    A. 2022

    B. 2018

    C. 2014

    D. 2010

10. Which artist featured Neymar in the hit "Pais do Futebol?"

    A. Michel Telo

    B. MC Guime

    C. Gustavo Lima

    D. Joao Carlos

10 Trivia Answers

1. C – Nike
2. D – 2020
3. B – February 2013
4. A – 0
5. C – 2012
6. D – 2019
7. B – 2020
8. C – Third
9. A – 2022
10. B – MC Guime

NEYMAR JR. CROSSWORD PUZZLE #2

ACROSS

[5] Sister's name

[7] First club

[8] Brand deal

[10] Middle name

DOWN

[1] Spanish club

[2] Place of birth

[3] Barcelona manager

[4] French club

[6] His profession

[9] National team

PUZZLE SOLUTIONS

NEYMAR JR. MAZE #1

NEYMAR JR. WORD SCRAMBLE #1

1. AZBILR OATNALNI TAEM ___ BRAZIL NATIONAL TEAM
2. OAJG NIBOOT ___ JOGA BONITO
3. EVFI SATR LILSKS ___ FIVE STAR SKILLS
4. PCONAMIHS GLAEUE ___ CHAMPIONS LEAGUE
5. EANYRM AD IAVLS SOSNAT NUIRJO ___ NEYMAR DA SILVA SANTOS JUNIOR
6. SPAINHS AL AGIL ___ SPANISH LA LIGA
7. ILUS EAUSZR ___ LUIS SUAREZ
8. LODRW UPC IALFN ___ WORLD CUP FINAL
9. SOEALEC BLAIRSIEAR ___ SELECAO BRASILEIRA
10. LONEIL IESSM ___ LIONEL MESSI
11. OMPLSICY ___ OLYMPICS
12. CF RNALEACOB ___ FC BARCELONA
13. SPAIR ISNTA EGANIRM ___ PARIS SAINT GERMAIN
14. DRNSAE SNIEATI ___ ANDRES INIESTA
15. IAVX ANEZNHDER ___ XAVI HERNANDEZ
16. UEILG NU ___ LIGUE UN
17. OSASNT CF ___ SANTOS FC
18. NOIODHLANR ___ RONALDINHO
19. IIVNUCIS OINURJ ___ VINICIUS JUNIOR
20. OCASV AD AAMG ___ VASCO DA GAMA

Neymar

NEYMAR JR. WORD SEARCH #1

N	A	J	O	G	A	B	O	N	I	T	O	M	A	Z
E	P	Q	L	P	C	E	C	F	T	S	D	S	G	I
Y	B	R	A	Z	B	R	A	Z	I	L	R	R	I	R
M	W	P	L	T	R	I	Q	W	U	O	I	Y	T	R
A	T	X	I	K	R	W	Q	O	P	T	B	C	M	R
R	M	Y	G	G	P	N	P	R	M	M	B	E	O	R
J	F	F	A	V	G	S	K	L	O	K	L	X	Q	U
R	U	Y	N	X	J	A	C	D	H	E	E	L	C	A
O	L	Y	M	P	I	C	S	C	A	N	R	G	G	W
K	S	K	I	L	L	S	Z	U	W	F	A	K	A	C
S	E	L	E	C	A	O	U	P	K	A	W	R	T	R
G	B	B	A	R	C	E	L	O	N	A	I	F	V	F
K	J	Q	K	T	C	W	X	Z	S	U	M	U	W	N
C	H	A	M	P	I	O	N	S	J	X	X	L	Q	Y
V	A	T	O	O	G	N	Q	U	P	V	Y	K	O	T

BRAZIL	CHAMPIONS	WORLDCUP	OLYMPICS
JOGABONITO	NEYMARJR	SELECAO	BARCELONA
SKILLS	LALIGA	MOHAWK	DRIBBLER

NEYMAR JR. WORD SCRAMBLE #2

1. ANRYEM RJ   NEYMAR JR
2. LAEABCNOR   BARCELONA
3. SPIRA N-GAASETMINR   PARIS SAINT-GERMAN
4. STNASO   SANTOS
5. EHRTIG-FOTDO   RIGHT-FOOTED
6. RDEEMIIFLD   MIDFIELDER
7. IRNEWG   WINGER
8. WDAFRRO   FORWARD
9. AZLIBR   BRAZIL
10. NRMLAIOILEI   MILLIONAIRE

NEYMAR JR. MAZE #2

NEYMAR JR. WORD SEARCH #2

```
W  Y  F  G  A  B  R  H  K  T  E  Y  F  P  U
B  B  A  U  T  Z  H  I  H  U  I  M  V  E  X
E  L  H  B  R  T  B  P  H  M  W  Y  A  B  G
E  N  R  R  A  I  N  I  E  S  T  A  S  W  G
G  D  Q  A  N  E  G  T  M  P  L  V  C  U  H
R  C  V  S  S  U  Z  H  E  Y  B  K  O  W  A
A  H  E  I  F  L  T  R  S  W  J  N  D  Z  V
V  Y  R  L  E  Y  G  Z  S  E  I  G  A  W  T
S  N  R  E  R  K  P  Z  I  F  P  W  G  U  K
U  G  A  I  F  R  S  A  N  T  O  S  A  W  E
A  F  T  R  E  L  A  S  P  K  U  F  M  P  N
R  T  T  A  E  L  I  G  U  E  U  N  A  E  D
E  K  I  O  B  R  R  P  E  N  A  L  T  Y  W
Z  D  J  J  R  O  N  A  L  D  I  N  H  O  F
Q  L  X  A  V  I  L  Q  J  I  Q  R  A  K  F
```

MESSI	RONALDINHO	BRASILEIRAO	VASCODAGAMA
VERRATTI	XAVI	SANTOS	LIGUEUN
SUAREZ	PENALTY	INIESTA	TRANSFERFEE

NEYMAR JR. WORD SCRAMBLE #3

1. AAAFELLR OTNASS   RAFAELLA SANTOS
2. NLOAARIC ASANDT   CAROLINA DANTAS
3. EDANNI OSCGEAVNL   NADINE GONCALVES
4. REAMNY RS   NEYMAR SR
5. CJIESAS RNIUIT   JESSICA TURINI
6. GMOI ASD CEUZRS   MOGI DAS CRUZES
7. IVAD CCAUL   DAVI LUCCA
8. OLAFBTLO   FOOTBALL
9. WDROL PUC   WORLD CUP
10. OAPC MCAIEAR   COPA AMERICA

NEYMAR JR. CROSSWORD PUZZLE #1

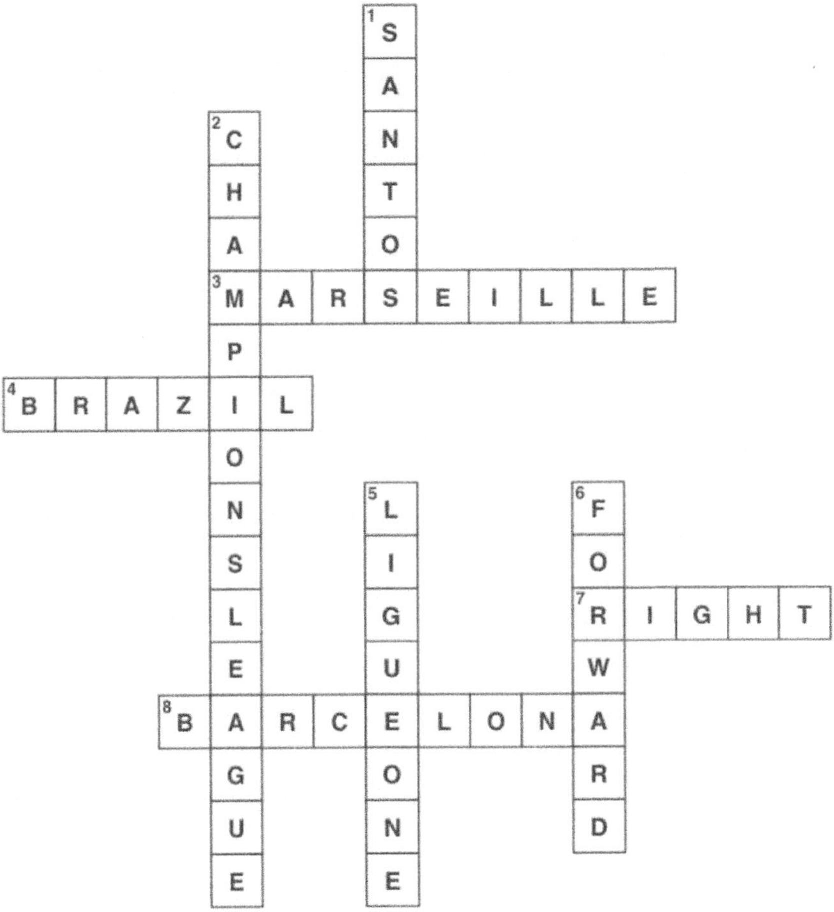

NEYMAR JR. WORD SEARCH #3

```
Z Y N I C F G U G J V I R F G
M P E L E R M B X N N Z A M A
E M S N B E X A Y U W T I Z R
J T Z P T E Y L G T F R N N J
G O S A X K R A Z M R J B J I
Y P T C H I J N K E A E O E Q
L S E E U C H C P G I F W N L
T C P S T K S E U G M I F M S
P O O O L E G E N D N V L E Q
S R V K T V Q Z G K L E I B G
P E E Z X H R Y L N O S C L V
E R R R M G Y S A G Z T K S M
E K S U I K V L F C C A I U O
D V B G O E H A L N R R W Q P
W L Y X G A V K U U D S N H B
```

RAINBOWFLICK   PELE   SPEED   STEPOVERS
LEGEND   FREEKICK   FIVESTARS   NUTMEG
BALANCE   MSN   PACE   TOPSCORER

NEYMAR JR. CROSSWORD PUZZLE #2

FINAL WHISTLE

Hello, our fellow footBaller.

We really hope you enjoyed *Neymar: The Complete Story of a Football Superstar*. And congratulations on reading it to the end!

We create these books to allow football fans to expand their knowledge around their favorite clubs and players, but most importantly, to keep the passion we all have for the game lit and alive.

Life can come with many challenges and setbacks. But something that never leaves our side is our love for the game.

If you enjoyed reading this book, we'd like to kindly ask for your feedback and thoughts in the review section on Amazon.

This would really encourage us to keep creating the highest quality books and content for football fans across the globe.

>>Scan the QR Code above to leave a short review on Amazon<<

Thanks in advance!

Ball out,

The House of Ballers team.

Made in the USA
Las Vegas, NV
31 January 2025